FIRST THINGS FIRST: ENSURING AUDITORY ACCESS

HELEN M. MORRISON, PH.D., CCC-A, LSLS CERT. AVT

RECIPE SLP

FIRST THINGS FIRST: ENSURING AUDITORY ACCESS

Copyright © 2015 Helen M. Morrison

This book is published by
Recipe SLP
Fort Worth, TX
http://www.recipeslp.com

ISBN: 978-1-941352-08-3

Cover design by Maria L. Muñoz
Formatting by Wild Seas Formatting (http://www.WildSeasFormatting.com)

Listening and Spoken Language Strategies for Young Children with Hearing Loss Series: Book 1

Contents

Introduction

First Things First: Ensuring Auditory Access and forthcoming books in the *Listening and Spoken Language Strategies for Young Children with Hearing Loss* series provide the how-to and evidence-base for strategies that help children with hearing loss learn to understand and use spoken language. Students and professionals (*e.g.*, speech-language pathologists, educators, audiologists, early interventionists) who work with young children with hearing loss will find the strategies in this series helpful and easy to apply in meeting intervention objectives. Parents can use the series as a resource for enhancing their child's language development.

What must be in place in order for a child with hearing loss to learn to understand and use spoken language? A reasonable response to this question might be a list that is informed by clinical experience and supported by research evidence (*e.g.*, Joint Commission on Infant Hearing, 2013); Sharma, Dorman & Spahr, 2002; Yoshinaga-Itano, 2003). It just might look something like this:

- early identification,
- early auditory access to the speech spectrum via hearing technology (*e.g.*, hearing aids, bone-anchored implants, cochlear implants),
- early enrollment in intervention, and
- active parent participation.

Now, imagine that you are a professional preparing to serve a family whose young child has a hearing loss. What must you **first** have in place in order to support that child's development of listening and spoken language? A hasty response to such a question might be the same list as above. The answer to this question, however, requires something more essential, more specific.

Optimal auditory access to spoken language via hearing technology must be in place first, so that auditory cortical development and spoken language acquisition can take place. For that reason, strategies that ensure auditory access establish the foundation upon which to base listening and spoken language intervention. The responsibility for ensuring that a child has auditory access to spoken language does not rest solely upon the child's audiologist at the time that devices are fit and programmed. Ensuring auditory access is a daily, even hourly, undertaking. All adults in a child's life bear responsibility for making it happen.

About this Book

First Things First: Ensuring Auditory Access describes six strategies that share the common purpose of ensuring that a child with hearing loss is receiving auditory access to spoken language with his hearing technology. The first strategy involves collecting and reviewing case records to verify that a child is participating in audiological management. The strategies that follow include suggestions for helping professionals interpret audiological records in order to plan and conduct intervention. The final strategies describe protocols to use at the start of each intervention session to ensure that hearing technology is operating as intended. Successful application of these strategies is more likely to be achieved when a collaborative relationship with the child's audiologist is established. Suggestions for creating a collaborative team are described. *First Things First* guides the reader in the development of six skills:

Strategy 1: Obtain complete and current audiological records.

Strategy 2: Be familiar with audiologic procedures recommended for assessing hearing in young children.

Strategy 3: Be familiar with audiologic procedures used to verify that hearing technology provides auditory access to the speech spectrum.

Strategy 4: Establish a collaborative relationship with the child's audiologist.

Strategy 5: Conduct daily checks of hearing technology and be prepared for problems.

Strategy 6: Conduct daily ear-specific Ling 6 Sound Tests.

The material in this book is organized to take you from reading about the strategies to putting them into practice. The following information is provided for each strategy.

Rationale: the relevance of the strategy to listening and spoken language development and intervention.

Description: a description of the strategy, including evidence for the effectiveness of the strategy.

Implementation: suggestions for implementation, including steps to follow and questions to ask yourself to help you identify your readiness for using the strategy.

References: full references for citations provided in Rationale and Description.

Resources: as needed, additional links and references to help you understand a strategy or to carry it out.

By applying strategies in your own setting, you are undertaking an approach to professional development that has proven to be effective for changing practice (Wilson, Houston & Nevins, 2010). You are free to implement the strategies that pertain to your particular level of expertise or are specific to the needs of a particular child.

At first reading, some strategies may appear to be written for audiologists rather than interventionists because they pertain to hearing and hearing technology. Not so! In order to ensure that a child has the auditory access to spoken language necessary for effective listening and spoken language intervention, the professional must have a basic knowledge of audiology and hearing technologies (A. G. Bell Academy, 2012a; Goldberg, Dickson & Flexer, 2010; Joint Committee on Infant Hearing, 2013, and be able to apply that knowledge into practice (A. G. Bell Academy, 2012b; Dickson, Morrison & Jones, 2014.

A Few Words About Words

The terms "professional," "parent," "intervention" and "he" are used in order to simplify the language in this book. "Professional" refers to any of the professionals who help children with hearing loss develop listening and spoken language: speech-language pathologists, educators, audiologists or early interventionists. "Parent" refers to any adult who assumes the role of caregiver in a child's life. "Intervention" pertains to therapy, home visits by a professional, or the classroom setting. Children with hearing loss are referred to as "he."

The Evidence Supporting These Strategies

The professions that serve children with hearing loss and their families employ a common approach to gathering evidence for effective practice (American Speech-Language-Hearing Association, 2004; Sackett et al., 1996. Three sources of evidence are used to judge the effectiveness of assessment and intervention strategies:

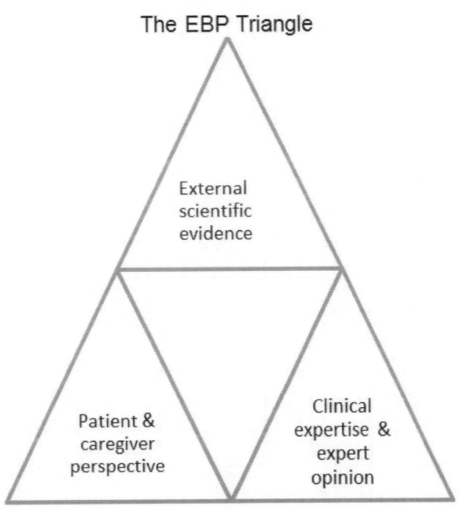

The EBP Triangle

Six documents supply the chief evidence for the strategies that are presented throughout this book, these include the following: the Joint Committee on Infant Hearing (JCIH) 2013 guidelines for early intervention and 4 clinical guidelines for pediatric audiological protocols developed by JCIH (2007), the American Academy of Audiology (AAA) (2012), (2013) and the Alexander Graham Bell Association for the Deaf (2014). The sixth document is a guide that outlines a 3-year plan for the development of professional skills that are essential for providing effective listening and spoken language intervention (Dickson, Morrison & Jones, 2014) used for the preparation of professionals who are working toward Listening and Spoken Language Specialist certification. These 6 documents were written by teams of recognized experts and include citations for external scientific evidence that support the recommendations, meeting criteria for first 2 out of the 3 types of evidence for effective clinical and educational practice.

Families and their children supply the third type of evidence for effective practice - client and caregiver perspectives. The families' needs, cultures, and perspectives provide the bases for selecting strategies and methods of implementation. JCIH (2013) calls for family-centered intervention that includes the parent/caregiver as an active participant. Research evidence indicates that when parents actively participate in intervention, greater benefit is achieved (Calderon, 2000; Yoshinaga-Itano, 2003). You, the reader, will collect this aspect of clinical evidence as you apply the strategies in this book in your practice and adapt strategies to the needs of families on your caseload.

References

American Speech-Language-Hearing Association. (2004). *Report of the Joint Coordinating Committee on Evidence-Based Practice.*
(http://www.asha.org/uploadedFiles/members/ebp/JCCEBPReport04.pdf#search="evi dence"))

A. G. Bell Academy for Listening and Spoken Language. (2012a). Core competencies/Domains of knowledge for the LSLS written examination. *Certification Handbook*. pp. 26-30.
(http://www.listeningandspokenlanguage.org/uploadedFiles/Get_Certified/Getting_Certified/Final 2012 Handbook.pdf)

A. G. Bell Academy for Listening and Spoken Language. (2012b). Mentor's observation and evaluation form. *Listening and Spoken Language Certified Auditory-Verbal Therapist 2012 Application*, pp. 22-26.
(http://www.listeningandspokenlanguage.org/uploadedFiles/Get_Certified/Getting_Certified/Editable AVT 2012.pdf)

A. G. Bell Association for the Deaf (2014). *Recommended Protocol for Audiological Assessment, Hearing Aid and Cochlear Implant Evaluation, and Follow-up.*
(http://www.listeningandspokenlanguage.org/Protocol.Audiological.Assessment/)

American Academy of Audiology (2012). *Audiologic Guidelines for the Assessment of Hearing in Infants and Young Children.*
(http://audiology-web.s3.amazonaws.com/migrated/201208_AudGuideAssessHear_youth.pdf_5399751b 249593.36017703.pdf)

American Academy of Audiology (2013). *Pediatric Amplification Guidelines.*
(http://audiology-web.s3.amazonaws.com/migrated/PediatricAmplificationGuidelines.pdf_539975b3e7e 9f1.74471798.pdf)

Calderon R. (2000). Parental involvement in deaf children's education programs as a predictor of child's language, early reading, and social-emotional development. Journal of Deaf Studies and Deaf Education, 5 (2):140–155.

Dickson, C. L., Morrison, H. M. & Jones, Mary, B. (2013). *The Mentor's Guide to Auditory-Verbal Competencies* (Years 1 – 3). Sydney: Cochlear Corporation.
(http://www.cochlear.com/wps/wcm/connect/74c238f5-887d-45a1-9f9b-66f2d53d9c6d/en_general _rehabilitationresources_mentorsguide_allyears_N530489-530492_iss1_sep14_1.76mb.pdf?MOD= AJPERES&CONVERT_TO=url&CACHEID=74c238f5-887d-45a1-9f9b-66f2d53d9c6d)

Goldberg, D., Dickson, C. & Flexer, C. (2010). AG Bell Academy certification program for Listening and

Spoken Language Specialists: Meeting a world-wide need for qualified professionals. *The Volta Review*, 110, 129-143.

Joint Committee on Infant Hearing (2007). Year 2007 position Statement: Principles and guidelines for early hearing detection and intervention programs. *Pediatrics*, 120 (4), 898-921. (http://pediatrics.aappublications.org/content/120/4/898.full.pdf+html)

Joint Committee on Infant Hearing (2013). Supplement to the 2007 position statement: Principles and guidelines for early intervention after confirmation that a child is deaf or hard of hearing. *Pediatrics*, 131l (4), 1324-1349. (http://pediatrics.aappublications.org/content/131/4/e1324.full.pdf+html)

Sackett, D. L., Rosenberg, W. M., Gray, J. A., Haynes, R. B. & Richardson, W. S. (1996). Evidence-based medicine: What it is and what it isn't. *British Medical Journal*, 312, pp. 71-72. (http://www.ncbi.nlm.nih.gov/pmc/articles/PMC2349778/pdf/bmj00524-0009.pdf)

Sharma A., Dorman M. F. & Spahr, A. J. (2002). A sensitive period for the development of the central auditory system in children with cochlear implants: Implications for age of implantation. *Ear and Hearing*, 23 (6):532–539.

Wilson, K., Houston, T. & Nevins, M. E. (2010). Professional development for in-service practitioners serving children who are deaf and hard of hearing. *The Volta Review*, 110 (2), 231-247.

Yoshinaga-Itano C. (2003). From screening to early identification and intervention: discovering predictors to successful outcomes for children with significant hearing loss. *Journal of Deaf Studies and Deaf Education*, 8, 11–30.

Strategy 1
Obtain complete and current audiological records.

Rationale

Planning listening and spoken language intervention without knowing what a child can hear is like driving blindfolded. It can lead to disaster! The audiological report is typically the first piece of information you will receive regarding how a child hears. Audiological assessments yield frequency-specific measures of what a child hears. Assessment of speech perception gives a view of how a child perceives the speech signal. This information allows you to predict which acoustic aspects of speech are most likely to be easiest for a child to detect and identify. As intervention proceeds, your ongoing observations and assessment of listening and spoken language will complement and validate audiological information.

The audiological report of assessment of hearing technology is likely to include the type, manufacturer, and model of the device(s) that a child is using. Knowing this will be helpful as you prepare for checks of the devices at the start of your sessions (Strategy 5).

The audiological record may also tell you when a child first received his hearing technology. This will tell you how long the child has had auditory access to spoken language, helpful for establishing expectations for the attainment of auditory developmental benchmarks. For example, expectations for auditory development will be different for a child who has been listening for 3 months and is just developing an awareness to sound, compared with a child who has been listening for 3 years and is listening to the conversations of his parents to learn about the world around him.

The Mentor's Guide to Auditory-Verbal Competencies (Dickson et al., 2013, p. 5), includes the following skills to be developed by professionals who are working toward Listening and Spoken Language Specialist (LSLS) certification, a 3-year process:

- Year 1: Obtains current audiological information for each child on caseload and adheres to the LSLS recommended audiological protocol.
- Year 2: Recognizes possible changes in child's audiological status and refers for assessment.
- Year 3: Coaches parents to monitor the child's auditory responses in order to seek audiological consultation as needed.

Description

Audiological records should include (AAA, 2012, 2013; A. G. Bell, 2014; JCIH, 2007):

- unaided or pre-implant audiogram,
- report of the child's auditory access to the speech spectrum using hearing technology, and
- assessment of each ear separately (unaided/pre-implant and with hearing technology), and date at which hearing technology was first fit.

Audiological records should be in the hands of the educator or clinician prior to or concurrent with enrollment in intervention (JCIH, 2013). Audiological assessments should continue to be conducted on a regular basis. Audiological assessments should be conducted regularly for several reasons:

- A child's participation in, and the thoroughness of, audiological assessment increases with developmental level (see also Strategy 2).
- Hearing can change.
- The functioning of a child's devices can deteriorate.
- Accordingly, the A. G. Bell Association (2014) and the JCIH (2007) recommend the following assessment schedule:
- When hearing loss is first diagnosed, every 4 to 6 weeks until complete audiograms are obtained.
- After the first complete audiogram is obtained, every 3 months through age 3 years.
- Age 4 years and older, every 6 months, *"if progress is satisfactory and if there are no concerns about changes in hearing"* (A. G. ,Bell, 2014)p. 2).
- If there is any concern about a change in hearing or breakdown in the child's devices, audiological assessment should be scheduled as soon as possible.

Implementation

Review your case records and look for the following:

- Unaided or pre-implant audiogram
    - left ear date: _____
    - right ear date: _____

- Date of first fitting with hearing technology: _____

- Assessment of hearing technology
    - left ear date: _____
    - right ear date: _____

- Do the dates of the reports indicate that the assessment schedule adheres to AAA, AG Bell and JCIH guidelines?

- Is there missing information?
- If there is missing information or a need for more current information:
    - contact the child's audiologist to see if there is additional information that can be supplied to you, and
    - refer the family for audiological assessment if current assessment is warranted.

References

A. G. Bell Association for the Deaf (2014). *Recommended Protocol for Audiological Assessment, Hearing Aid and Cochlear Implant Evaluation, and Follow-up.* (http://www.listeningandspokenlanguage.org/Protocol.Audiological.Assessment/)

American Academy of Audiology (2012). *Audiologic Guidelines for the Assessment of Hearing in Infants and Young Children.*

American Academy of Audiology (2013). *Pediatric Amplification Guidelines.*
*(http://audiology-web.s3.amazonaws.com/migrated/201208_AudGuideAssessHear_youth.pdf_*
5399751b249593.36017703.pdf)

Dickson, C. L., Morrison, H. M. & Jones, Mary, B. (2013). *The Mentor's Guide to Auditory-Verbal*
Competencies (Years 1 – 3). Sydney: Cochlear Corporation.
(http://audiology-web.s3.amazonaws.com/migrated/PediatricAmplificationGuidelines.pdf_
539975b3e7e9f1.74471798.pdf)

Joint Committee on Infant Hearing (2007). Year 2007 position Statement: Principles and guidelines for
early hearing detection and intervention programs. *Pediatrics, 120* (4), 898-921.
(http://pediatrics.aappublications.org/content/120/4/898.full.pdf+html)

Joint Committee on Infant Hearing (2013). Supplement to the 2007 position statement: Principles and
guidelines for early intervention after confirmation that a child is deaf or hard of hearing. *Pediatrics, 131I*
(4), 1324-1349.
(http://pediatrics.aappublications.org/content/131/4/e1324.full.pdf+html)

Resources

Visit Recipe SLP to download a sample records review form.

(http://www.recipeslp.com/books.html)

Strategy 2
Be familiar with audiologic procedures recommended for assessing hearing in young children.

Rationale

Once you collect audiological reports, you must be able to understand what the audiologist is reporting and why. This will enable you to counsel parents and to apply audiological information to intervention planning and implementation.

One might suppose that it is the audiologist's job to explain the audiological assessment results to parents. But think back to the time that you were first learning about audiology and audiological procedures. How many times did you need to encounter the information before you understood it fully? Parents need the same repeated opportunities to learn and understand. You have far more frequent contact with parents than does the child's audiologist and have opportunities during sessions to show the relevance of audiological information to the child's listening development.

You will also be helping children and their parents prepare for the tasks that a child is expected to perform in audiological assessment. When a child is prepared for audiometry the efficiency of assessment is improved and the amount of information that can be obtained increases. For an example, consider these educator/clinician goals from *The Mentor's Guide* (Dickson et al., 2013, p. 5) for LSLS aspirants:

- Year 1: Collaborates with audiologist to develop or choose child's tasks to be used in audiological assessment/ hearing technology programming.

- Year 2: Prepares child for audiological assessment/hearing technology programming, including establishing play audiometry skills when appropriate, and shares observations about child's speech perception.

- Year 3: Assists parents in sharing their observations with their audiologist regarding the child's speech perception.

Description

Pediatric audiologists can assess infant hearing as early as birth. A newborn responds to sound differently, however, than does an older infant or a preschooler. Audiologists must use assessments that are compatible with a child's developmental level in order to obtain the most reliable information possible. For that reason, audiological guidelines recommend different assessment protocols for different child developmental levels (AAA, 2012; A. G. Bell, 2014; JCIH, 2007) in order to obtain an audiogram. Not only are different audiological procedures recommended for different age levels but the results of these various audiological procedures will be reported using different terminology.

Summary of Recommended Protocols

The recommended audiological protocols for infants and young children fall into 3 categories.

- **Physiological assessment** of auditory system function which does not require the child to perform a task.

- **Behavioral assessment** enables the audiologist to observe a child's response to sound.
- **Speech perception assessment** measures a child's response to speech. This includes the determination of the softest speech intensity a child can hear and the calculation of the accuracy of a child's recognition of words *(e.g.* via imitation or pointing to pictures).

Pediatric audiologists use a number of procedures to measure auditory thresholds (the softest sounds that a child can hear) and speech recognition. The procedures recommended at several age groups are listed in the table below. We'll refer to this table as we explore some of the issues that arise in testing children, how you can help parents understand audiological reports, and how you can assist the audiologist. Some of these procedures may be unfamiliar to you and will be described briefly below. The Resources at the end of this strategy provide additional information. The Ling 6 Sounds are described in Strategy 6.

Age/ Developmental Level	Physiological Assessment	Behavioral Assessment 250 - 8000 Hz	Speech Perception
0 - 6 months	Auditory Brainstem Response (ABR) Auditory Steady State Response (ASSR)	Observation of orienting responses	Observation of orienting to Ling 6 sounds
6 - 12 months	ABR ASSR	Visual Reinforcement Audiometry (VRA)	Detection of Ling 6 sounds with VRA
12 - 24 months		VRA	Speech reception threshold (SRT) Word recognition (Using simple vocabulary)
24 – 36 months		Conditioned play audiometry (CPA)	SRT Word recognition (Using simple vocabulary)
> 36 months		CPA	SRT Word recognition (Using standardized materials)

Recommended Protocols for Infants

Audiologists pair physiological assessment with behavioral and speech perception assessment of infants from birth through 12 months in order to balance the strengths and limitations of each protocol.

1. Behavioral Assessment

Orienting responses (i.e., movement in response to an external stimulus such as a sound) are observed from the youngest infants. Orienting responses include eye shifts, head turns, or changes in the rate at which an infant sucks from his bottle. The loudness at which a child makes an orienting responses is not considered to be a true auditory threshold because infants at this age tend to require sound that is higher than the softest that can be heard in order to respond (AAA, 2012; Hicks, Tharpe & Ashmead, 2000). Nevertheless, observation of orienting responses can provide information about general auditory responsiveness to a variety of sounds across frequencies and to speech. Audiological reports of this sort of behavioral observation will describe a child's responses as **orienting responses** and will report the lowest intensities across frequencies (or speech) at which responses were observed.

The pediatric audiologist administers **Visual Reinforcement Audiometry**, or VRA, to older infants by pairing sound with an interesting visual display such as a cartoon on a computer screen until the infant is conditioned to expect the cartoon when he hears a sound. The audiologist knows that an infant is conditioned when the audiologist presents sound without the visual display and the infant looks around for source of the sound. The intensity levels at which a conditioned response can be obtained vary with the age of the child (Sabo, Paradise, Kurs-Lasky & Smith, 2003). As a consequence, responses to sound obtained with VRA are not considered to be true auditory thresholds but do have a "close, predictive relationship to auditory thresholds" (AAA, 2012, p. 12). Audiological reports of VRA testing will describe a child's responses as **minimum response levels**, reporting the lowest intensities across frequencies (or speech) at which conditioned responses were obtained.

2. Physiological Assessment

Behavioral testing of infants is time consuming, often requiring multiple visits in order to obtain a picture of how well an infant responds to speech and the frequencies across the range of 250 through 8000 Hz. In contrast, the physiological assessments ABR and ASSR provide objective results without behavioral response and are typically more efficient, providing frequency-specific information within only one or possibly two appointments.

The Auditory Brainstem Response (ABR) and Auditory Steady State Response (ASSR) are electrical potentials that are generated by the cochlea and auditory nerve in response to sound. Electrodes placed on the child enable a computerized system to detect these potentials. Infants and children must be asleep or sedated for the testing. The sounds used in the ABR test include clicks and tone bursts. Clicks stimulate the auditory system in the range of 2000 to 4000 Hz. ABR tone bursts can be centered around 500, 1000, 2000 or 4000 Hz. ASSR uses tonal stimuli as well and can provide a bit wider frequency and intensity range.

There are limitations to what ABR can tell us, due to signal limitations. Click stimuli are limited to the 2000 to 4000 Hz region. If an infant's auditory system does not respond to a click, it does not mean that the infant is unable to respond to all sound frequencies but merely indicates a deficit in hearing in the 2000 to 4000 Hz range. There is also an intensity limit to ABR stimuli, generally 85 - 90 dBHL. If an infant's auditory threshold is 95dB HL the test stimulus cannot evoke a response from the infant's auditory system. In this case, for example, the audiological report may say that there was "no response to 85 dBHL tone pip at 1000 Hz." Just as a "no response" to a click does not necessarily mean that an infant is unable to respond to all sound, so also does a "no response" to an 85 dBHL signal mean that an infant is unable to hear. It simply means that an infant is unable to hear a signal that is 85dBHL or softer. Parents are often dismayed when they receive an ABR report that says "no response." Your knowledge and explanation can be of great help.

Thresholds obtained via ABR or ASSR fall within 5 to 20 dB of auditory thresholds, depending upon the procedure and stimuli (Stapells, 2011). As a consequence, audiologists typically apply a correction to the thresholds obtained by ABR and ASSR to better estimate auditory thresholds. The audiological report will indicate the signal used in testing, the lowest intensity that evoked a response, and if a correction factor was applied (AAA, 2013).

Recommended Protocols for Toddlers and Preschoolers

Conditioned play audiometry (CPA) is generally recommended for ages 2 and above. CPA is the classic block dropping task, i.e., child drops block in response to hearing a tone. The audiologist varies the tone intensity until auditory threshold is determined. The key to successful CPA is having the child demonstrate a consistent response to sound. This can be taught and can be taught in a way that is fun.

Parents can be coached to practice this task at home.

Although CPA is not recommended as an audiological procedure until a child is 2 years old, it is possible to begin to expose a child to elements of the task prior to the second birthday if the child is developmentally ready. When a child starts to imitate what you and parents are doing in the session, you can model detection responses to sound. Training suggestions appear below in the Implementation section.

When a child begins to understand words, he can begin to participate in word-based speech perception assessment. You and the child's parents can assist the audiologist by supplying the audiologist with a list of words that a child understands. The child's audiologists may have toys or pictures of simple vocabulary that they prefer to use. Obtain a list of these words and include them in your sessions in order to familiarize the child.

Recommended Protocols for Ages 3 and Above

Guidelines for speech perception testing with this age group recommend the use of "standardized materials." These standardized materials are published word lists and associated pictures that have been standardized by research for use with specific age groups. The Resources section below gives references for a few of the word lists that pediatric audiologists use with young children.

When you find out which materials a child's audiologist uses, you and the child's parents can review the words to identify what the child knows. Speech perception testing is not vocabulary testing so using words that a child understands increases test accuracy. You can assist audiologists by alerting them to words that a child does not understand. You can also incorporate test words into language experiences so that the child's vocabulary includes the words that he may encounter during audiological assessment.

Implementation

Audiological Assessment Review Questions

Review each child's audiological assessments. Answer the questions listed below as you read each report.

- Do you know how to read an audiogram?
    - If not, make this a priority for your professional development. Start with How to Read an Audiogram in the Resources section below.

- Do you understand the terminology used in the report?
    - If not, look over the resources at the end of this section. Get in touch with the child's audiologist and ask for an explanation.

- How was the child assessed?

- What frequencies were tested?

- What are the thresholds or minimum response levels at the frequencies assessed?

- What is the minimum intensity at which speech is detected?

- Was the child's ability to understand speech assessed at a level above the speech threshold? How?

- What materials were used?

- Do you know what words are included in the materials?

- Are there any concerns about child's knowledge of the words in the speech materials?

- Is there any information that may be missing?

- Are you able you explain the results to the child's parents?
  - If not, locate resources to help you and/or contact the child's audiologist to help you better understand the information.

Prepare Children and Parents for Play Audiometry

Prior to an audiological assessment, contact the child's audiologist to find out what task the child is expected to perform in play audiometry. Tell the audiologist what you have observed regarding the child's ability to respond to a sound. Use this information to guide your plan for training the child. Don't forget to update the audiologist as the child learns to respond to an auditory stimulus!

Teach the child to display a consistent observable response to sound. To begin, when you and parents hear a sound, point to your ear and say, "I hear that!" Take the child to the source of the sound and repeat the sound and response (if possible). Encourage the child to begin to point to his ear as well.

Look for signs that the child is ready to start learning the structured detection task that is CPA. Will the child imitate your actions? Will the child follow a simple command with a gesture (e.g. "Put it in." when you want the child to place a block in a bucket.)?

Start training with speech as the stimulus rather than a less familiar tonal stimulus. Use a meaningful phrase that is appropriate to the task: "Put it in, put it on, drop it, etc."

Start with hand-over-hand with the parent giving the command and you guiding the child.

Include a block-dropping task or other detection task in each session until a consistent response to sound is established. Coach the parents and child to drop blocks and a bucket, stack rings on a stick, drop small objects in a vase filled with water in response to hearing "put it in" or a Ling 6 Sound (Strategy 6). See the description of tasks for Strategy 6 for more detail regarding obtaining a detection response.

Keep it brief. Remember that this is *teaching* not testing hearing. Stop before it gets boring.

Coach parents as they try the task with their child so that they can practice play tasks at home.

Prepare Children and Parents for Speech Perception Testing

With parents, maintain a list of the early words that a child understands and communicate this to the audiologist prior to assessment.

Find out from the audiologist what test materials will be used. The audiologist might be able to scan or fax a copy of the word list for you. Let the audiologist know if there are any words that a child doesn't understand. Include items from the list in language experiences to help build the child's ability to participate in speech recognition testing.

Brainstorm with parents for ways to include test words in daily experiences for child acquisition. The words used in pediatric speech recognition are common everyday words that can be easily highlighted in home language. For example, the spondees used for speech threshold testing often include words such as ice cream, cupcake, toothpaste, and bathtub.

References

A. G. Bell Association for the Deaf (2014). *Recommended Protocol for Audiological Assessment, Hearing Aid and Cochlear Implant Evaluation, and Follow-up.*
(http://www.listeningandspokenlanguage.org/Protocol.Audiological.Assessment/)

American Academy of Audiology (2012). *Audiologic Guidelines for the Assessment of Hearing in Infants and Young Children.*
(http://audiology-web.s3.amazonaws.com/migrated/201208_AudGuideAssessHear_youth.pdf_5399751b249593.36017703.pdf)

American Academy of Audiology (2013). *Pediatric Amplification Guidelines.*
(http://audiology-web.s3.amazonaws.com/migrated/PediatricAmplificationGuidelines.pdf_539975b3e7e9f1.74471798.pdf)

Dickson, C. L., Morrison, H. M. & Jones, Mary, B. (2013). *The Mentor's Guide to Auditory-Verbal Competencies (Years 1 – 3).* Sydney: Cochlear Corporation.
(http://www.cochlear.com/wps/wcm/connect/74c238f5-887d-45a1-9f9b-66f2d53d9c6d/en_general_rehabilitationresources_mentorsguide_allyears_N530489-530492_iss1_sep14_1.76mb.pdf?MOD=AJPERES&CONVERT_TO=url&CACHEID=74c238f5-887d-45a1-9f9b-66f2d53d9c6d)

Hicks, C.B., Tharpe, A. M., Ashmead, D. H. (2000). Behavioral auditory assessment of young infants: Methodological limitations or natural lack of auditory responsiveness? *American Journal of Audiology*, 9 (2), pp. 124-130.

Joint Committee on Infant Hearing (2007). Year 2007 position statement: Principles and guidelines for early hearing detection and intervention programs. *Pediatrics*, 120 (4), 898-921.
(http://pediatrics.aappublications.org/content/120/4/898.full.pdf+html)

Sabo, D. L., Paradise, J. L., Kurs-Lasky, M., Smith, C. G. (2003). Hearing levels in infants and young children in relation to testing technique, age group, and the presence or absence of middle-ear effusion. *Ear and Hearing*, (24), 38-47.

Stapells, D.R. (2011). Frequency-specific threshold assessment in young infants using the transient ABR and the brainstem ASSR. In R.C. Seewald and A.M. Tharpe (eds.), *Comprehensive Handbook of Pediatric Audiology* (pp.409-448). San Diego: Plural Publishing, Inc.

Resources

A. G. Bell Association for the Deaf (2014). *Recommended Protocol for Audiological Assessment, Hearing Aid and Cochlear Implant Evaluation, and Follow-up.* Recommended audiological speech test protocols by age of child, pp. 1-12. (Includes links for obtaining word lists used in different speech tests.)
(http://www.listeningandspokenlanguage.org/Protocol.Audiological.Assessment/)

American Speech-Language Hearing Association: Types of Tests Used to Evaluate Hearing in Children and Adults
(http://www.asha.org/public/hearing/Types-of-Tests-Used-to-Evaluate-Hearing/).

Boystown National Research Hospital: My Baby's Hearing: Hearing tests to expect as your child grows
(http://www.babyhearing.org/HearingAmplification/HearingLoss/testsexpect.asp).

First Years, How to Read an Audiogram
(http://www.firstyears.org/lib/howtoread.htm).

Kimbell, S. H. & Meyers, A. D. Pediatric speech materials. Medscape. (http://emedicine.medscape.com/article/1822315-overview#a30)

Madell, J.R. and Flexer, C. (2008). *Pediatric Audiology: Diagnosis, Technology and Management*. NY: Thieme.

Madell, J.R. and Flexer, C. (2011). *Pediatric Audiology Casebook*. NY: Thieme.

Visit Recipe SLP to download a sample records review form. (http://www.recipeslp.com/books.html)

YouTube: If you are unfamiliar with any of the audiological procedures described in this Strategy, look them up on YouTube for a visual demonstration. The supply of videos is constantly growing so specific links are not included here.

Strategy 3
Be familiar with audiologic procedures used to verify that hearing technology provides auditory access to the speech spectrum.

Rationale

When you are planning and conducting intervention, a fundamental question is, "What can the child hear?" You need this information to apply the most appropriate sensory strategies for facilitating listening and spoken language development. The question of what a child can hear is actually a question about how well a child can access speech while listening with hearing technology. The unaided audiogram does not fully tell you what you need to know. You need the information that the audiologist obtains when assessing hearing technology performance.

Audiologists use different kinds of procedures to assess different kinds of hearing technology. And just as the child's developmental level drives audiometric assessment, so does child development have bearing on the protocols used to assess hearing technology. Understanding these protocols will help you to interpret the results with regard to the child's ability to hear with his technology. It will also help you counsel the child's family.

Pediatric audiologists use checklists, rating scales, and questionnaires that supplement audiological information with information from families and interventionists about how the child is listening with his technology in the real world. Familiarity with some of these tools will help make your observations more efficient and your communication with the audiologist more effective.

The Auditory-Verbal competencies outlined in *The Mentor's Guide*), (Dickson et al., 2013, p. 5)) for Strategy 2 apply to this strategy as well:

- Year 1: Collaborates with audiologist to develop or choose child's tasks to be used in audiological assessment/ hearing technology programming.

- Year 2: Prepares child for audiological assessment/hearing technology programming, including establishing play audiometry skills when appropriate, and shares observations about child's speech perception.

- Year 3: Assists parents in sharing their observations with their audiologist regarding the child's speech perception

Description

The goal of fitting with hearing technology is to make the acoustic speech spectrum (or, simply speech) audible to the child. Audiologists use a variety of approaches to verify that they have achieved this goal. The type of hearing technology that the listener wears will dictate just how the audiologist conducts verification.

Hearing Aids

1. Real ear and simulated real ear measures.

The American Academy of Audiology (2013) recommends 2 approaches for verifying that a child has acoustic access to speech with his hearing aids. The first is the real-ear aided response (REAR) probe microphone method. The second is a simulation of the REAR called the "real-ear to coupler difference"

(RECD) method.

In the REAR approach, the audiologist places a tiny probe microphone in the child's ear canal and then places the hearing aid into the ear. A complex sound that replicates the speech signal is delivered through a loudspeaker to the hearing aid. The probe microphone picks up the sound emitted by the hearing aid in the child's ear canal and transmits that sound to a computer for analysis. Computer software compares the measures obtained from the hearing aid to values that have been determined to be desirable for a child to be able to hear and understand speech (also known as "targets") (Ching *et al.*, 2010). The audiological report of REAR hearing aid assessment is likely to have language that says something like, "Probe microphone measurements indicate that the hearing aid fitting reaches targets" or "reaches the desired levels."

The REAR method requires that a child be able to sit very still while the probe microphone is placed in his ear canal and hearing aid output is measured. This is not easy for infants and young children! The RECD approach avoids the challenge of keeping a young child still. Rather than placing the hearing aid and probe microphone in a child's ear, the audiologist attaches the hearing aid to a metal cylinder that substitutes for the ear canal. The hearing aid and cylinder are then placed in a hearing aid test box with a microphone placed at the end of the cylinder. A speech-like signal is sent to the hearing aid in the test box. Sound travels from the hearing aid through the cylinder to the microphone. The microphone transmits the sound emitted by hearing aid to a computer for analysis.

Before analysis of sound from the hearing aid can begin, however, the computer first makes an adjustment for differences between the size of the metal cylinder and the size of young children's ear canals. These adjusted hearing aid output measures are then compared to targets in the same manner as the REAR approach described above. The audiologist's report employs similar language as with the REAR approach, *e.g.* "Simulated probe microphone measurements using the RECD approach indicate that the hearing aid fitting reaches targets" or "reaches the desired levels".

Computerized probe microphone protocols can produce a graph that compares the output of the hearing aid to the targets necessary for auditory access to spoken language. This kind of graph can show how audible speech is for each of the frequencies in the speech range, enabling some prediction regarding which aspects of speech (suprasegmentals, vowels, consonants) will be more or less audible to the child. Typically this graph is not included in audiological reports. You can request a copy from the audiologist and ask the audiologist to walk you through an interpretation of the information.

2. Aided soundfield audiograms.

You are likely to have soundfield aided audiograms among your audiological reports. These audiograms are obtained by testing a child in the sound booth while wearing his hearing aids using developmentally appropriate protocols (*e.g.* observation of orienting responses, VRA, conditioned play; see Strategy 2). The sounds that are used for testing are delivered through loudspeakers. The audiologist may plot the unaided and aided audiogram on the same form to provide a comparison between the two listening conditions. There may be a conversational speech spectrum sketched on the audiogram, also known as the "speech banana" (a link to a description of the speech banana appears in the Resources section below). Audiologists often use the aided soundfield audiogram as a counseling tool to demonstrate how the child hears with and without hearing aids, and to illustrate which aspects of speech are audible with hearing aids.

The aided soundfield audiogram is *not*, however, the preferred approach for hearing aid assessment in any of the guidelines published by the JCIH (2007), AAA (2013) or A. G. Bell Association (2014). Audiologists are urged to move away from use of the aided audiogram as a means to verify that hearing aids provide acoustic access to the speech spectrum. The rationales and scientific evidence against the use the aided soundfield audiogram can be found in the 2013 AAA guidelines (pp. 39-40). Three general statements summarize the rationales. First, today's digital hearing aids amplify quiet, conversational and loud speech levels differently. The aided soundfield audiogram cannot demonstrate how the hearing aid handles these different speech levels. Second, the relatively simple signals used to obtain aided soundfield audiograms fail to demonstrate how digital hearing aids respond to the complex and fast-changing signal that is speech and can misrepresent aided benefit. And finally, the aided soundfield audiogram fails to display the performance of the hearing aid at frequencies that fall between the octaves on the audiogram form. There is much information that is lost when performance at these intermediate frequencies is not displayed. The implication for listening and spoken language intervention is that the aided soundfield audiogram fails to give a fully accurate picture of how the hearing aid provides acoustic access to the speech spectrum.

Nevertheless, real ear or simulated real ear measures fail to tell us how the individual child responds to sound while wearing his hearing aids. The aided soundfield audiogram and the observations that the audiologist makes while obtaining the soundfield audiogram do give that information. Ideally, the pediatric audiologist will obtain both real ear and aided soundfield measures.

3. Aided speech perception testing.

Guidelines do recommend conducting aided soundfield speech perception assessment using protocols and speech materials that are matched to the child's developmental and language level (see also Strategy 2). You can help the child's audiologist assess speech perception by circumventing the possible impact of the child's language ability on the testing using the suggestions in Strategy 2.

Bone-Anchored Implants (BAI) and Cochlear Implants

Unlike hearing aids, the output of BAIs and cochlear implants cannot be measured directly when coupled to the child. And, unlike hearing aids, guidelines do recommend obtaining a soundfield audiogram with the child wearing the BAI or cochlear implant using developmentally appropriate protocols (see Strategy 2) and speech stimuli appropriate for the child's language level.

Outcomes Assessment: Functional Assessment of Hearing Technology

Audiological protocols verify that a child's hearing technology provides access to the acoustic speech spectrum. Outcomes assessments use parent and interventionist reports to evaluate a child's functional use of hearing technology. These checklists, questionnaires, and rating scales serve to validate that technology fitting is successful by confirming that technology is helping the child in real world situations, including listening in noisy environments and at a distance (AAA, 2013). The AAA Guidelines (2013), pp. 41-45) list reporting tools for different age ranges that have normative data. Sources and descriptions for some of these tools appear in the Resources section below. It is helpful to find out if a child's audiologist uses specific checklists or questionnaires, and to obtain copies of what the audiologist uses. You can use the checklists to coach parents to observe their child's responses to sound in the home. You can also complete a checklist on your own, reporting the child's responsiveness with hearing technology in the intervention setting so that the audiologist has a report of listening in more than one environment.

One note about these checklists and questionnaires. Many items on these tools give an indication of a child's listening development and performance that can be used by you for intervention planning and implementation. They may not, however, give you all the information you will need for intervention planning. Consider these tools to be just a first look at a child's auditory ability. More in-depth assessment strategies for use by educators and clinicians will be described in a later volume in this series.

Frequency of Hearing Technology Assessment

The various Guidelines are less specific regarding the recommended frequency of hearing technology assessment compared with guidelines for audiological assessment of hearing. In general, the following statements can be made.

When assessing a child wearing hearing aids, use (at a minimum) the same test intervals recommended for audiological assessment:

- When hearing aids are first fit: every 4 to 6 weeks until full assessment of aided hearing is obtained,

- After the first complete assessment of aided hearing: every 3 months through age 3 years,

- Age 4 years and older: every 6 months if progress is satisfactory and there are no concerns about changes in hearing or the hearing aids.

For children wearing cochlear implants/BAI, consult the audiologist about the scheduling for the assessment of implanted technology. The A. G. Bell Academy Guidelines (2014) recommend checks each 3 months during the first year of cochlear implant use, and each 6 to 12 months in subsequent years if progress is satisfactory.

If there is any concern about the function of hearing technology, the audiologist should be contacted ASAP.

Implementation

Questions to Answer as You Read a Hearing Technology Assessment Report

- Is there a current assessment of hearing technology?
  - If not, ask parents how recently technology was assessed.
  - If hearing technology was assessed recently, obtain a copy of the report.
  - If it has not been assessed recently, refer parents to the pediatric audiologist for an assessment.

- How was the child's hearing technology assessed?
  - Do you understand the terminology used in the report?
  - If not, look over the resources at the end of this section. Get in touch with the child's audiologist and ask for an explanation.

- If a child wears hearing aids, were aided real ear or simulated real ear measures obtained?
  - Was a printout showing the output of the hearing aids included in the report?
  - If not, contact the audiologist and ask if the audiologist might supply a copy and talk you through interpretation of the information.

- Was a sound field audiogram obtained with the child wearing hearing technology?
  - What frequencies were tested?
  - What are the thresholds or minimum response levels at the frequencies assessed?

- Can you interpret the soundfield audiogram with regard to which acoustic aspects of speech are most audible to the child?
  - If not, refer to the resources below for additional information.

- Was speech perception assessed with the child wearing hearing technology?
  - What is the minimum intensity at which speech is detected?
  - Was the child's ability to understand speech assessed at a level above the speech threshold? How?
  - What materials were used?
  - Do you know what words are included in the materials?

- Are you able you explain the results to the child's parents?
  - If not, locate resources to help you and/or contact the child's audiologist to help you better understand the information.

- Does the audiologist provide the family a checklist or other material for reporting how their child uses his hearing technology in real environments?

- If the answer to the last question was **yes**, ask yourself:
  - Is there a copy of the form and results in the report?
  - Is the family in the process of completing the form? If yes, have the family bring the form to the session so you can coach parents and refer to the items on the form when reporting your observations of the child's listening to parents during the session.
  - Contact the audiologist and request a copy of the form or a link to a copy. Use the form to report your observations of the child in the session.

- If the answer to the last question was **no**:
  - Contact the audiologist and ask what sort of information is helpful for you and parents to report regarding the child's use of hearing technology in the real world.
  - Look over the Resources for Outcomes/Functional Assessments in the Resources section and choose some to try out in your practice. Coach parents to use them as well. Parents can bring this information to the hearing technology assessment.

Prepare the Child for Hearing Technology Testing

If there are any concerns about the child's knowledge of the words in the speech materials let the audiologist know about words that are not in the child's vocabulary. Teach the child any words that might be important to know in the assessment.

Prepare children and parents for play audiometry to be conducted with hearing technology. See suggestions in Strategy 2 for implementation.

Prepare children for speech recognition testing using hearing technology. See suggestions in Strategy 2 for implementation.

References

A. G. Bell Association for the Deaf (2014). *Recommended Protocol for Audiological Assessment, Hearing Aid and Cochlear Implant Evaluation, and Follow-up.*
(http://www.listeningandspokenlanguage.org/Protocol.Audiological.Assessment/)

American Academy of Audiology (2013). *Pediatric Amplification Guidelines.*
(http://audiology-web.s3.amazonaws.com/migrated/PediatricAmplificationGuidelines.pdf_539975b3e
7e9f1.74471798.pdf)

Ching, T.Y.C., Scollie, S.D., Dillon, H., Seewald, R.C., Britton, L., Steinberg, J., Gilliver, M. & King, K. (2010). Evaluation of the NAL-NL1 and the DSL v.4.1 prescriptions for children: paired-comparison judgments and functional performance ratings. *International Journal of Audiology. 49* (Suppl. 1) S35-48.

Dickson, C. L., Morrison, H. M. & Jones, Mary, B. (2013). *The Mentor's Guide to Auditory-Verbal Competencies (Years 1 – 3).* Sydney: Cochlear Corporation.
(http://www.cochlear.com/wps/wcm/connect/74c238f5-887d-45a1-9f9b-66f2d53d9c6d/en_general
_rehabilitationresources_mentorsguide_allyears_N530489-530492_iss1_sep14_1.76mb.pdf?
MOD=AJPERES&CONVERT_TO=url&CACHEID=74c238f5-887d-45a1-9f9b-66f2d53d9c6d)

Joint Committee on Infant Hearing (2007). Year 2007 position Statement: Principles and guidelines for early hearing detection and intervention programs. *Pediatrics, 120* (4), 898-921.
(http://pediatrics.aappublications.org/content/120/4/898.full.pdf+html)

Resources

Advanced Bionices: IT-MAIS: Infant-Toddler Meaningful Auditory Integration Scale
(https://www.advancedbionics.com/content/dam/ab/Global/en_ce/documents/libraries/AssessmentTools/
AB_IT-MAIS_Resource.pdf).

Boystown National Research Hospital: My Baby's Hearing: How is a hearing aid tested on a baby or a young child?
(http://www.babyhearing.org/HearingAmplification/AidChoices/evaluated.asp)

First Years: The Speech Banana
(http://www.firstyears.org/lib/banana.htm)

Madell, J. R. (2011). Pediatric amplification: Using speech perception to achieve best outcomes. *Audiology Online,* February 7, 2011.
(http://www.audiologyonline.com/articles/pediatric-amplification-using-speech-perception-841)

Millet, P. D. Understanding your student's aided hearing using the Desired Sensation Level approach. Success for Kids with Hearing Loss.
(http://successforkidswithhearingloss.com/understanding-student-aided-hearing)

Oticon (2005). COW – The Children's Outcome Worksheets
(http://www.pro.oticonusa.com/~asset/cache.ashx?id=10833&type=14&format=web).

Oticon (2005): Incorporating Functional Auditory Measures into Pediatric Practice.
(http://www.pro.oticonusa.com/~asset/cache.ashx?id=10831&type=14&format=web)

Oticon (2007). CHILD – Children's Home Inventory.
(http://www.pro.oticonusa.com/~asset/cache.ashx?id=10831&type=14&format=web)

Visit Recipe SLP for a records review form.
(http://www.recipeslp.com/books.html)

Strategy 4
Establish a collaborative relationship with the child's audiologist.

Rationale

Listening and spoken language cannot develop optimally without auditory access to spoken language, and auditory access depends upon optimal audiological management. Optimal audiological management best proceeds when there is an easy and effective collaboration among the audiologist, family, and educator/clinician.

Optimal management of a child with hearing loss is a team effort involving the family, the audiologist, professionals who address listening and spoken language development, and professionals who help parents address additional challenges (*e.g.* occupational and physical therapists). The JCIH (2013) specifies that team members should "work as an effective and integrated member of a trans-disciplinary team, in a manner that optimizes child and family learning" (p. 1332).

The following Auditory-Verbal competencies outlined in *The Mentor's Guide* (Dickson et al., 2013, p. 22) apply to this strategy:

- Year 1: Establishes positive working relationships with parents and colleagues.

- Year 2: Develops working relationships with all members of the team surrounding children on caseload.

- Year 3: Creates a relationship of mutual respect within the team and wider community when dealing with difficult people.

Description

The key word in this strategy is **collaboration**. The task of creating a collaborative relationship with a child's audiologist is two-fold: (1) establishing a collaboration across varied professional disciplines and (2) establishing a collaboration within the complexities of each professional's responsibilities and schedule demands. The first requires communication, respect, empathy, and education. The second requires logistics.

Professionals who work with children with hearing loss - audiologists, speech-language pathologists and educators - apply common knowledge and skills regarding development, speech and language, hearing, and hearing technology on a daily basis (A. G. Bell Academy, 2012). Nevertheless, each profession has its own particular area of expertise and language that is used in daily practice. In order to communicate effectively across professions it is helpful to have some knowledge of the work that each does and the language used to describe that work. The concepts in Strategies 2 and 3 are examples of what professionals who are not audiologists might want to understand when communicating with audiologists.

It is helpful to keep in mind that the audiological practice guidelines that inform the strategies in this book are not mandated standards. You are likely to discover that audiologists work in ways that vary from practice guidelines for clinically valid reasons, including the child's developmental level, presenting health issues, or family needs (AAA, 2013).

Diplomacy is powerful when establishing a collaboration. It may be necessary to communicate to the audiologist those aspects of auditory perception that are of concern, including a description of the possible frequency regions that the child appears to be having trouble perceiving. For example, if a child consistently confuses /i/ and /u/, you might report this and indicate that you have concerns about acoustic access in the frequency region around 2000 Hz (see Strategy 6). Nevertheless, it is neither realistic nor helpful to direct the audiologist to re-program the hearing aid or implant to provide better response at 2000 Hz in this case. Typically, the solution for difficulties in speech perception is not a simple matter of turning up the aids or re-MAPing the implants at a specific frequency. The audiologist is best assisted with several examples of the types of word or speech sound confusions that are observed and whether or not these are observed consistently or if the difficulty varies over time.

Despite differences in scope of practice that exist among members of the collaborative team, effective teamwork can be achieved by recognizing that team members have a common focus on helping the child and family (IPEC, 2011). When we keep the focus on the needs of the child and family, we are less inclined to focus on our own needs or on perceived shortcomings of other team members. We are more likely to come up with solutions in a constructive, respectful manner.

The greatest challenge to collaboration with a child's audiologist may be finding the time to make this happen (IPEC, 2011). It's unlikely that you and the child's audiologist share common times that are free for meetings. It's likely that you are attempting to establish a working relationship with several audiologists since the children on your caseload may be managed by different audiologists, exacerbating the difficulty in finding times for phone conversations, much less face-to-face meetings. Nevertheless, it is possible to establish collaboration in other ways, such as by email. Each time contact is established, the professional relationship has an opportunity to grow.

Implementation

Review your case records. Do you have the name and contact information for each child's audiologist? Do you have releases signed by the family giving you permission to contact the audiologist? If not, obtain contact information and releases.

Call or send an email to each child's audiologist. Introduce yourself. Establish that you value the audiologist's contribution and that you can be counted upon to be a partner in helping the child learn to use hearing technology to the fullest.

Find out the audiologist's preferred method of communication. Phone? Email? Skype or Facetime? What are the constraints in your setting and the audiologist's with regard to communication media and patient privacy?

Find out what the audiologist would consider to be helpful information from you to help prepare for assessment or to document progress.

Create a form that the parents can take to the audiologist at the time of assessment. You and the parents can complete the form prior to the appointment to provide updated information on the child's current level of auditory functioning, vocabulary that might be helpful for speech perception testing, and any concerns that you or the family might have. Provide space on the form for the audiologist to quickly jot down any reply or new information.

It may be helpful to schedule a standing meeting for case management, such as a monthly phone conversation, if you have several children who are seeing the same audiologist; particularly if these children are newly implanted or new hearing aid users. If you have scheduled a monthly conversation in advance you can make note of what you want to talk about during the weeks prior to the meeting and cover that in one conversation. If there is nothing to discuss that month, you can always cancel the meeting. Cancelling is always easier than trying to find a time to meet!

Show your appreciation. Say it with chocolate, or at least a thank you note.

References

A. G. Bell Academy for Listening and Spoken Language. (2012). Core competencies/Domains of knowledge for the LSLS written examination. *Certification Handbook.* pp. 26-30. (http://www.listeningandspokenlanguage.org/uploadedFiles/Get_Certified/Getting_Certified/Final 2012 Handbook.pdf)

American Academy of Audiology (2013). *Pediatric Amplification Guidelines.* (http://audiology-web.s3.amazonaws.com/migrated/PediatricAmplificationGuidelines.pdf_539975b3e7e 9f1.74471798.pdf)

Dickson, C. L., Morrison, H. M. & Jones, Mary, B. (2013). *The Mentor's Guide to Auditory-Verbal Competencies (Years 1 – 3).* Sydney: Cochlear Corporation. (http://www.cochlear.com/wps/wcm/connect/74c238f5-887d-45a1-9f9b-66f2d53d9c6d/en_general_ rehabilitationresources_mentorsguide_allyears_N530489-530492_iss1_sep14_1.76mb.pdf?MOD= AJPERES&CONVERT_TO=url&CACHEID=74c238f5-887d-45a1-9f9b-66f2d53d9c6d)

Interprofessional Education Collaborative Expert Panel (IPEC) (2011). *Core competencies for interprofessional collaborative practice: Report of an expert panel.* Washington, D.C.: Interprofessional Education Collaborative. (http://www.aacn.nche.edu/education-resources/ipecreport.pdf)

Joint Committee on Infant Hearing (2013). Supplement to the 2007 position statement: Principles and guidelines for early intervention after confirmation that a child is deaf or hard of hearing. *Pediatrics, 131I* (4), 1324-1349. (http://pediatrics.aappublications.org/content/131/4/e1324.full.pdf+html)

Strategy 5
Conduct daily checks of hearing technology.

Rationale

If hearing technology is not working, it is impossible for a child to have full auditory access to speech. And technology can break down at any given moment! Even if a parent reports that the devices were checked earlier in the day, you must conduct an equipment check at the start of each session. Checking devices at the start of each session will model a habit that should be in place at home as well.

If you are not checking the device because it takes time away from teaching and therapy, consider this: time spent trying to learn and listen through non-working devices is a greater loss than a short wait for a device check. The more you check, the speedier and more effective you'll become.

The following Auditory-Verbal competencies outlined in *The Mentor's Guide* (Dickson et al., 2013, p. 5) apply to this strategy:

- Year 1: Checks hearing aids/cochlear implants/personal FM, etc. at the start of each session. Troubleshoots hearing aids/cochlear implants/personal FM, etc. and communicates issues/solutions effectively to parents and child's audiologist.

- Year 2: Assists parents to daily check and troubleshoot hearing aids, cochlear implants, and personal FM.

- Year 3: Assists parents to devise a method to keep track of the status of hearing aids, cochlear implants, and personal FM.

Description

Hearing technology is the strongest link to facilitating auditory access to spoken language for children with hearing loss. It is also the weakest link. Hearing aids, for example, have a long history of breakdowns. Researchers who checked hearing aids in preschool and school-age settings at various times throughout the school day discovered problems at rates ranging from 30-70% with little improvement in results observed over almost 50 years (Gaeth, 1966; Zink, 1972; Elfenbein, 1994; Burkhalter, Blalock, Herring & Skaar, 2011). These were issues that could be identified via listening and visual checks. Parents and professionals must be constantly vigilant to ensure that hearing technology is providing the intended benefit.

Hearing aids can be checked directly by listening to them using either a hearing aid stethoscope or a custom fit earmold attached to a listening tube. You can purchase hearing aid stethoscopes online or from an audiologist. Audiologists can make an impression of your ear and facilitate the purchase of a custom earmold. If you are not familiar with listening checks, ask an audiologist to show you how or look over the Resources below.

A different approach is needed for listening to BAI's. You can connect the BAI speech processor to a Softband or a test rod, hold the processor against your skull (forehead or mastoid process), plug your ears and listen to the bone conducted sound. Earplugs are preferred for shutting out air conducted environmental sound, rather than your fingers, because plugs can block out a greater amount of sound and your hands are free to handle the BAI. A Softband or test rod can be obtained through the child's audiologist or the BAHA manufacturer. The manufacturer provides user manuals and videos that can be helpful.

It is not possible to conduct direct listening checks of cochlear implants. You can conduct a visual check of the external components and any LED lights that indicate processor function. The external components and LED indicators will vary by manufacturer and model. Cochlear implant manufacturer websites provide downloadable guides for educators/clinicians and videos that can help you navigate checks and troubleshooting.

It is helpful to have the manufacturer and model of your clients' devices. This information may be in the audiological report, or you may need to request this. When you have this information you can go to manufacturers' websites and download user manuals for these devices. User manuals can help you understand how to troubleshoot the device and to recognize any warning LED's or sounds that the device emits when something goes wrong.

Implementation

Keep in mind that each piece of hearing technology will be a little different, depending upon the type of technology, the manufacturer, and the model. It is beyond the scope of this volume to walk the reader through a check of every possible form of technology that a professional will encounter. You have a number of resources available to assist you if you haven't conducted a check for a particular type of technology.

- Ask for a demonstration from a colleague, the parents, or the child's audiologist.
- Obtain the user or professional manual from the manufacturer's website (see *Resources* below).
- Search for YouTube demonstrations.

Listen to and Examine **Hearing Aids or BAIs** at the Start of Each Session.

Obtain the necessary equipment for each type of technology:

Purchase a hearing aid stethoscope from an audiologist or online (see *Resources* below). Or have an audiologist make an impression of your ear for a listening tube.

Contact the implant audiologist to obtain a test rod for a child's BAI (see *Resources* below).

Keep the earmold on the hearing aid when you attach it to the stethoscope or listening tube for a listening check. Removing the earmold stretches the tubing and it can then become easily detached from the hearing aid.

Use the Ling 6 Sounds when you listen so that you can listen to the devices using sounds across the frequency range of speech (see Strategy 6).

A time-saving hint: Don't take out the battery of the hearing aid or BAI to check it until you've listened. If the device sounds fine, no need to remove the battery for a check. This is especially helpful when you are dealing with child-protected battery cases.

At the Start of Each Session Conduct a Visual Check of the **Cochlear Implants**.

Have the child's parents guide you through the way they check their child's devices. This will help you understand the device if it is new to you. It will also tell you what parents understand about device checks and provide insight regarding any coaching that they might need.

What to do if the Technology is not Working.

If the technology is not working, troubleshoot to determine the source of the problem. Be prepared to replace dead batteries or broken cords. Coach parents to keep a supply of batteries and cords (if appropriate) with them at all times so that these can be replaced.

If technology problems cannot be ameliorated, use the session time for parents to make an appointment with the child's audiologist for audiological check and repair, to catch up on parent concerns, and to coach parents in communication strategies when a child is not hearing optimally.

References

Burkhalter, C.L., Blalock, L., Herring, H. & Skaar, D. (2011). Hearing aid functioning in the preschool setting: Stepping back in time? *International Journal of Pediatric Otorhinolaryngology*, 75 (6), 801 – 804.

Dickson, C. L., Morrison, H. M. & Jones, Mary, B. (2013). *The Mentor's Guide to Auditory-Verbal Competencies (Years 1 – 3)*. Sydney: Cochlear Corporation. (http://www.cochlear.com/wps/wcm/connect/74c238f5-887d-45a1-9f9b-66f2d53d9c6d/en_general _rehabilitationresources_mentorsguide_allyears_N530489-530492_iss1_sep14_1.76mb.pdf?MOD= AJPERES&CONVERT_TO=url&CACHEID=74c238f5-887d-45a1-9f9b-66f2d53d9c6d)

Elfenbein, J. (1994). Monitoring preschoolers' hearing aids: issues in program design and implementation, *Am. J. Audiol. 3*, 65–70.

Gaeth, J. H. & Lounsbury, E. (1966). Hearing aids and children in elementary schools, *J. Speech Hear Disord. 31* (3), 283–289.

Zink, G. D. (1972). Hearing aids children wear: a longitudinal study of performance, *Volta Rev. 74* (1), 41–51.

Resources

Hearing aid check information and demonstrations:
Alexander Graham Bell Association
(http://www.listeningandspokenlanguage.org/hearingaidtest.aspx)

National Center for Hearing Assessment and Management (NCHAM)
(http://www.infanthearing.org/videos/featured/hearing_aid_listening_check.php)

Hearing aid stethoscopes:
Westone
(http://www.westone.com/store/index.php/professional-supplies/stethoscopes.html)

Samples of hearing aid user guides:
Oticon
(http://www.oticonusa.com/product-showcase.aspx)

Phonak
(http://www.phonak.com/com/b2c/en/support/support.html)

Samples of implant user guides:
Advanced Bionics
(http://www.oticonusa.com/product-showcase.aspx)

Cochlear Corporation
http://www.cochlear.com/wps/wcm/connect/us/recipients/nucleus-5/nucleus-5-basics/user-manuals-and-videos)

Med El
(http://www.medel.com/us/user-support-us/)

Strategy 6
Conduct ear-specific Ling 6 Sound Tests daily.

Rationale

Conducting a Ling 6 Sound Test (Ling, 1988, 2003, 2013) at the start of each session enables you to quickly identify changes from one week to the next so that problems with the child's device or his hearing (such as otitis media or progression in hearing loss) can be investigated and managed. It is especially important to conduct a Ling 6 sound test at the start of a session with children who are listening through cochlear implants because you are unable to hear the signal that is being delivered to the implanted child to confirm that all is well.

The following Auditory-Verbal competencies outlined in *The Mentor's Guide* (Dickson et al., 2013, p. 6) apply to this strategy:

- Year 1: Conducts a Ling 6 sound test at the start of each session.

- Year 2: Conducts Ling 6 sound test using tasks appropriate to child's level of auditory function (detection, identification, etc.). Interprets responses to the Ling 6 sound test based on child's aided/implanted information and speech acoustics.

- Year 3: Communicates child's responses of Ling 6 sound test to parents and child's audiologist in an effective manner.

Description

The Ling 6 Sounds, /m/, /u/, /i/, /a/, /ʃ/, and /s/, are phonemes produced in isolation that encompass the frequency and intensity range of speech. Knowing how well a child can detect the Ling 6 sounds and how well a child can discriminate one sound from another tells us how well a child is able to access the conversational speech spectrum.

There are 3 types of child responses that can be elicited in the Ling 6 Sound test, based on the developmental level and auditory skill of the child.

- Detection: A child drops a block, stacks rings on a stick, or performs some other simple action in response to hearing a Ling sound. This response demonstrates that a child can hear the syllable presented, but fails to indicate whether auditory access is sufficient to make each syllable distinct from one another.

- Discrimination/Imitation: A child imitates the phoneme that he hears. This requires that the child be able to produce the phonemes clearly enough that you and his parents know what he has perceived.

- Identification: A child points to a picture or picks up an object that represents the phoneme. This requires teaching the child to associate the sound with the object or picture. An internet search can locate pictures for the Ling 6 Sound test on cochlear implant and hearing aid manufacturers' websites. Some sources are provided in the *Resources* section below.

Each sound should be presented separately as a brief syllable, about the same duration that phonemes appear in spoken language:

"mmmm" "ooooo" "eeeee" "aahhh" "shhhh" "sssss"

Some children may require longer phoneme durations when they are first starting out.

The Ling 6 Sound Test is a check of audition so lipreading should not be made available. Presentation from the side or behind the child avoids providing lipreading cues. Ideally, the Ling 6 Sound test should be conducted close to the child and at distances of 3 and 10 feet in order to verify the distance that the child hears well (Ling, 2003, 2013). The Ling 6 Sound Test should be conducted with the child wearing his hearing device and one ear at a time. If you only conduct the test with the child wearing devices on both ears, you might miss discovering that one of the devices is not working.

The table below displays the frequency in Hz of energy peaks of each of the Ling 6 sounds, using information supplied by Ling (1988, 2003, 2013) and organized according to audiometric frequencies. The absolute frequencies of the Ling sounds vary with a speaker's age and gender. The frequencies in speech produced by an adult male, for example, are lower than those produced by a 3 year-old child. As a consequence, the frequencies listed below represent a range extending from ½ octave below to ½ octave above the frequency heading each column.

Ling Sound	Primary Frequencies (± ½ octave)					
	250 Hz	500 Hz	1000 Hz	2000 Hz	4000 Hz	6000 Hz
/m/	X					
/u/	X (F1)		X (F2)			
/i/	X (F1)			X (F2)		
/a/			X			
/ʃ/				X		
/s/					X	

Notice how the sounds appear across the table. Some have peak energy at lower frequencies, some at higher. Some sounds have peak energy at more than one frequency. For example, both the first (F1) and second (F2) formants for the vowels /u/ and /i/ appear on the table. Notice also that some sounds have peak energy at the same frequencies. For example, /m/, /u/ and /i/ all have energy at 250 Hz, although in application the energy in the consonant /m/ extends to just below 250 Hz and the energy in /u/ and /i/ extends to within the frequency range between 250 and 500 Hz.

You can use the table to interpret a child's responses to the Ling 6 Sound test based on a the child's ability to detect a sound or discriminate between sounds.

For example, if a child fails to detect:

- /m/: There may be inadequate auditory access in the low frequencies (250 Hz and below).
- /ʃ/ and /s/: There may be inadequate auditory access in the high frequencies (2000 Hz and above).
- /s/: There may be inadequate auditory access in the very high frequencies (4000 Hz and above).
- Any of the sounds *except* /a/: The child is only hearing the strongest speech sound, /a/, and hearing only the mid-frequency range of speech.
- Additionally, if a child fails to discriminate:
- /u/ *from* /i/: There may be inadequate auditory access above 1000 Hz.
- /ʃ/ *from* /s/: There may be inadequate auditory access above 2000 Hz.

The test should only take a few minutes at the start of the session. Young children who are in the early weeks of intervention may require some time learning to produce a consistent detection response or to imitate a phoneme. These are skills that underlie the acquisition of listening and spoken language so time spent learning these skills is not time wasted.

Implementation

Right after you check the child's hearing technology (see Strategy 5), conduct an ear-specific Ling 6 Sound test at the start of the session. Conduct the test close to the child and at distances (3 and 10 feet away).

Choose a task that is consistent with the child's developmental and auditory skill level. Spend time in the session training for the task and moving the child to the next level, but do not make Ling 6 training and testing the primary focus of the listening and spoken language session.

Keep track of how the child responds from week to week. Have the parent contact the child's audiologist if changes in response are seen.

References

Dickson, C. L., Morrison, H. M. & Jones, Mary, B. (2013). *The Mentor's Guide to Auditory-Verbal Competencies (Years 1 – 3)*. Sydney: Cochlear Corporation. (http://www.cochlear.com/wps/wcm/connect/74c238f5-887d-45a1-9f9b-66f2d53d9c6d/en_general_ rehabilitationresources_mentorsguide_allyears_N530489-530492_iss1_sep14_1.76mb.pdf?MOD= AJPERES&CONVERT_TO=url&CACHEID=74c238f5-887d-45a1-9f9b-66f2d53d9c6d)

Ling, D. (1988). Foundations of Spoken Language for Hearing-Impaired Children. Washington, D. C.: A. G. Bell.

Ling, D. (2003). The six sound test. In W. Estabrooks & L. Birkenshaw-Fleming (Eds.) *Songs for Learning! Songs for Life!* Washington, D. C.: A. G. Bell., pp. 227-229.

Ling, D. (2013). What is the Six-Sound Test and why is it so important in Auditory-Verbal therapy and education? In W. Estabrooks (Ed.) *101 Frequently Asked Questions About Auditory-Verbal Practice.* Washington, D. C.: A. G. Bell, pp. 58-62.

Resources

Advanced Bionics Tools for Schools Ling 6 Sound Check description (http://www.advancedbionics.com/content/dam/ab/Global/en_ce/documents/libraries/AssessmentTools/3-01066-B-1_Ling Six Sound Check-FNL.pdf)

Advanced Bionics Ling 6 Sound Test printable flashcards (http://www.advancedbionics.com/content/dam/ab/Global/en_ce/documents/libraries/AssessmentTools/3-01066-B-9_Ling Six flash cards-FNL.pdf)

Cochlear Corporation Ling 6 Sound Test description and sample forms for documenting responses over time (http://hope.cochlearamericas.com/sites/default/files/HOPE/Ling-6_sound_test-how_to.pdf)

Cochlear Corporation printable Ling 6 Sound Test cards (http://hope.cochlearamericas.com/listening-tools/ling-6-sounds)

Cochlear Corporation Speech Acoustics Made Easy (http://hope.cochlearamericas.com/sites/default/files/resources/speech_acoustics_made_easy.pdf)

Summary

The strategies in this book encompass the knowledge base and habits that must be in place to help ensure that a child has the acoustic access necessary for cortical auditory development and spoken language acquisition. Some strategies can be observed in the everyday conduct of an intervention program – maintaining records, communicating with the child's audiologist, and starting each session with an equipment check and ear-specific Ling 6 Sound Test. Others are less visible, but just as important. For example, establishing the knowledge base required for interpretation of audiological information should a priority if one is to work with children with hearing loss and their families. Maintaining that knowledge base continues throughout one's career as technology and scientific understanding of human audition advance.

It is often the case that a child and his family begin intervention without all the audiological information that the professional might desire. Sometimes it is not possible to establish easy communication with a child's audiologist. Equipment breaks down. As a professional, you may feel that you have gaps in your knowledge base. None of these situations, however, justifies postponing or stopping intervention. These situations do justify diligence in problem-solving to ameliorate deficiencies. If one does not have complete audiological information regarding acoustic access with hearing technology, for example, child responses to the Ling 6 Sounds give the professional a great deal of information regarding how well the child's technology helps him.

You are off to a great start but there is much more to learn. The strategies in this book are fundamental for setting up and starting an intervention session; next up is the real "meat" of intervention – setting goals, teaching, coaching parents. The volumes that follow in this series will include models for assessment and development of audition, spoken language, speech production and parent coaching. The *First Things* have been put into place. We are ready to start the listening and spoken language journey.

About Recipe SLP

Recipe SLP, EBP how-to for SLPs, is the speech-language pathologist's source for affordable guides to the science and practice behind clinical procedures for managing communication impairments across the lifespan. We examine the literature in order to report the purpose, target population, and foundational steps for each procedure. Additionally, we explain variations and modifications that can expand the usefulness of the procedure. Based on our own clinical experience, we provide tips, suggestions, and sample exchanges to help clinicians feel confident when implementing the treatment procedures. Each guide includes a brief up-to-date summary of the evidence supporting each treatment and a bibliography with active links to online research articles, conference presentations, and relevant websites.

Recipe SLP is committed to helping speech-language pathologists transfer knowledge between science and practice. Our books summarize the methods and evidence for procedures used by speech-language pathologists to address communication challenges resulting from impairments in speech, language, and cognition across the lifespan. Recipe SLP values culturally relevant practice in speech-language pathology and considers the applicability of the clinical procedures for culturally and linguistically diverse populations.

We would love to hear from you!

Visit our website http://www.recipeslp.com
Like us on Facebook https://www.facebook.com/recipeSLP
Follow us on Twitter https://twitter.com/RecipeSLP
Read our blog http://recipeslp.wordpress.com/

More books by Recipe SLP
The Aphasia Series
The Clinician's Guide to Semantic Feature Analysis
The Clinician's Guide to Reducing Aphasic Perseveration
The Aphasia Series Vol. 1: SFA, RET, RAP

Purchase eBooks through from your favorite online book store

PDFs and other formats available at Smashwords
(https://www.smashwords.com/books/search?query=RecipeSLP).

Print-on-demand available through Amazon (http://www.amazon.com/Maria-L-Munoz/e/B00IY2JQMO/ref=dp_byline_cont_book_1).

About the Author

Helen M. Morrison, Ph.D., CCC-A, LSLS Cert. AVT has over 40 years of experience as an educator of children with hearing loss, an audiologist, and Auditory-Verbal Therapist. Dr. Morrison earned her B.A. in deaf education at Trinity University in San Antonio, Texas, her M.S. in audiology at the U. of Oklahoma Health Sciences Center in Oklahoma City and her Ph.D. in speech communication at The University of Texas at Austin. She has worked in hospitals, schools, universities and in private practice. Prior to retirement in 2012, Dr. Morrison was an Associate Professor at Texas Christian University for 17 years, teaching courses and supervising students in both education of the deaf and hard of hearing and in speech-language pathology. Her research focused on early vocal behaviors by children with hearing loss and on evidence-based practice patterns by Auditory-Verbal Therapists. Her work has been published in a number of peer-reviewed journals including *Clinical Linguistics and Phonetics, Journal of the Acoustical Society of America, Journal of the American Academy of Rehabilitative Audiology, Journal of Educational Audiology, Journal of Speech and Hearing Research,* and *The Volta Review.*

Dr. Morrison is currently mentoring professionals across the United States who are working toward Listening and Spoken Language Specialist certification. She teaches online courses globally in skill development for professionals who are looking for evidence-based strategies to increase children's listening and spoken language. She is a co-author of *The Mentor's Guide to Auditory-Verbal Competencies (Years 1 – 3)*. Dr. Morrison was awarded the *Dallas Business Journal* Health Care Hero award in 2010 for her work in continuing education for professionals in evidence-based strategies for listening and spoken language development.

Made in the USA
Lexington, KY
03 January 2018